This Greenbird Book
belongs to

First published in Great Britain in 2012 by Greenbird Books
Text © 2012 by Safiyya Bintali
Illustrations © 2012 by Daniela Frongia
This book has been typeset in Palatino Linotype
Printed in USA

British Library Cataloguing in Publication Data:
A catalogue record for this book is available from the
British Library.

ISBN:978-0-9571995-21

www.greenbirdbooks.com

Notes for parents and teachers

This short story book was published in an effort to raise awareness about autism within Muslim communities. It has been written from the perspective of a young sibling, who has explained this cause with a gentleness and simplicity, which will be easily understood.

There are countless resources available for more information on autism and how families can be supported. Special recognition goes to Safiyya's mother for maintaining a valuable online blog resource, *My Autistic Muslim Child*.

The below is taken from the Holy Qur'aan in an effort to explain the infinite bounty of blessings bestowed upon us by our creator, *Allah* Almighty.

And among His Signs is the creation of the heavens and the earth, and the variations in your languages and your colours: verily in that are Signs for those who know. *(Roman:22)*

This book is dedicated to my brother Amin, who touched my life in so many ways. Also, I dedicate this book to my mom, dad and all the siblings and caretakers of children who have autism to remind them, not to lose the sight of the possible reward that they may achieve in the Hereafter.

Safiyya

Have you ever wondered how you would express yourself if you didn't know how to talk?

Have you ever imagined the world without any communication? Not knowing what your loved ones feel, to express where you hurt, or what you want?

Were you ever in a foreign country, not speaking their language, not knowing what they say?

There are only a few questions you need to consider when you meet a child who has autism and cannot talk.

Children with autism feel like they are in a foreign country, and can't understand things. So, we should treat them nicely, firmly, and make them feel at home.

Help the children with autism open doors to a new world. Help them rise over the rocks. Make these children live in peace, alongside everyone.

You could say, "How are you?"... This question shows that you care.

Some children with autism are scared, because they think people will hurt them. Sometimes because they are scared we don't understand their behaviour. We need to remember they are a blessing from *Allah* (God), and we should help them to not be scared.

You have to be patient, gentle, and kind to children with autism. Then you might help them to become more independent, or *high-functioning* like my brother, Amin.

Children with autism have the rights to do everything, just like you and me. They can make their bed, tie their shoes, put on clothes, make a sandwich, and much more.

Children with autism need to be treated like royalty! All kids are special, but children like my brother need extra care. Usually when you meet such a child, hold out your hand and say "hello".

Children who cannot speak are *Allah*'s (God's) creation. Even my brother Amin, who is almost eight years old and very strong, feels pain and hurt just like you and me.

He is *high-functioning* because we took him out into the world.

Can you imagine being the sibling of a person of *Jannah* (Paradise)? Well, I am one of those persons. I am Amins' sister, Safiyya.

Can you imagine on the Day of Judgment these children will be asking *Allah* (God) to increase your rewards for all the sacrifices you made for them?

My brother is a person of *Jannah* (Paradise), and he is a very huge blessing for me and my family.

Sometimes in the back seat of my car, I really can't believe this valuable human is sitting next to me, playing his video games!

He is a wonder and a reminder to us all that *Allah* (God) has made us all different, equal and special. We are very fortunate to have Amin in our lives and I wanted to share this message with you all.

About the Author

Safiyya Bintali

Safiyya was nine years old at the time of writing this book. She is a sister, a friend and a teacher to an eight years old little boy, Amin. The inspiration to write this book came from her learning all about her brother Amin, who has autism.

She's been home-schooling since 1st grade, and has taken many online writing courses. Her dream is to become a journalist, so she can use the media effectively to raise awareness about autism.

She is also a passionate animal lover and one of her dreams is to have a farm with her best friend when she grows up. Greenbird Books is delighted to be working with such an inspiring individual and seeks to actively promote the awareness of autism in Muslim communities.

For further information please visit **www.greenbirdbooks.com**

Greenbird Books
Children's Book Publisher

www.greenbirdbooks.com

www.ingramcontent.com/pod-product-compliance
Lightning Source LLC
Chambersburg PA
CBHW040022050426
42452CB00002B/100